September 11th, The Day

Jesus Christ Was Born

By

Tony Ray

The scripture used throughout this book is quoted from the KING JAMES Version of the Bible unless otherwise noted.

On September 11, 3 B.C. sunset was at 6:18 pm and moonset at 7:39 pm. It was during this eighty-one minute period of time that Jesus Christ was born in Bethlehem of Judaea. In this booklet, September 11th the Day Jesus Christ was born, Tony Ray presents a thorough and careful examination of astronomical, secular, and biblical records that pre-date the horrific attack on the United States of America, on 9/11. When read carefully, the evidence presented in this book, will help you to determine precisely and conclusively, that September 11th, 3 B.C. was the day Jesus Christ was born!

In memory of my mother,

Gloria Stokes Ray

October 3, 1929 – September 11, 1979

ACKNOWLEDGEMENT

This book , *September 11th, The Day Jesus Was Born*, would not be possible, without the great research team Victor Paul Wierwille put together in August of 1979, to help him with his book, *Jesus Christ Our Promised Seed* published in 1982.

ASTRONOMY AND THE BIBLE

Ancient literature will help one to begin to understand how the heavens, the stars and planets reveal God's plan of Redemption for mankind. But how can we begin to know and understand what the stars and planets reveal to us about God's plan.

The Bible says in **Psalms 147:4**, "*He (GOD) telleth (counted) the number of the stars, he calleth them all by their names.*" When God created the heavens and the earth in the beginning, He gave specific names to all of the stars. He made them, He knows how many there are, and calls each of them by a specific name.

God taught Adam the names of the stars, the constellations and how the heavens reveal aspects of His marvelous plan of redemption. Adam in turned shared this knowledge, which was passed on for centuries.

In other words, God's plan of redemption, according to the stars, planets, constellations and their positioning existed thousands of years before this information was given in written form.

Let's take a look at **Psalms 19:1-6** –"*The heavens declare the glory of God and the firmament sheweth his handy work". Day unto day uttereth speech and night unto night sheweth knowledge. There is no speech nor language, where their voice is heard. Their line is gone out through all the earth, and their words to the end of the world. In them hath he set a tabernacle for the sun. Which is as a bridegroom coming out of his chamber, and rejoiceth as a strongman to run a race. His going forth is from the end of the heaven, and his circuit unto the ends of it: and there is nothing hid from the heat thereof.*"This particular passage of scripture clearly indicates that the 'heavens declare God's glory, they show knowledge, and set forth His purposes'.

Genesis 1:14 says, "*And God said, Let there be lights in the firmament of heaven to divide the day from the night and let them be for signs and for seasons and for days and years.*"

The word "signs" in **Genesis 1:14** derives from the Hebrew word *avah*. *Avah* means "to mark". It is used of marking someone significant to come. So we see, that right at the very beginning of the Bible, in the book of Genesis, God reveals the lights in the firmament of the heavens are signs of significant things to come.

That helps us to realize that **Genesis 1:14** points to the prophecy of the one spoken of in **Genesis 3:15**, the "seed of the woman", Jesus Christ the Messiah.

Genesis 3:15 says, "*And I will put enmity between thee and the woman, and between thy seed and her seed, it shall bruise thy head, and thou shalt bruise his heel*". When properly understood, the stars, planets, and constellations reveal God's divine plans.

Unfortunately, the original God-given revelation of celestial signs and events, and the way that they influence human history has been perverted. Biblical astronomy and astrology are vastly different. Astrology, which supposedly interprets the influence of the stars and planets on people lives corrupts and perverts the original and true meaning of the stars' revelation of God's divine plans. The Bible forbids astrology and worship of celestial bodies, **Isaiah 47:12-14** says, "*...stand now with thine enchantment, and with the multitude of thy sorceries, wherein thou hast labored from thy youth. If so be thou shalt be able to profit if so be thou mayest prevail? Thou art wearied in the multitude of thy counsels. Let now the astrologers, the stargazers, and the monthly prognosticator stand up, and save thee from these things that shall come upon thee.*

Behold, they shall be as stubble the fire shall burn them, they shall not deliver themselves from the power of the flame. There shall not be a coal to warm at, nor fire to sit before it."

The study of the Bible and astronomy provides one the true knowledge and understanding of the stars, in relation to the coming of the One who is the Christ.

Throughout ancient history, the twelve constellations were known to depict and reveal eternal truths. For example, Jacob in **Genesis 49: 9-10,** while on his death bed, prophesies concerning his twelve sons and their offspring. Here are the words, to his son Judah, "*Judah is a lion's whelp: from the prey, my son, thou art gone up: he stooped down, he couched as a lion, and as an old hen, who shall rouse him up? The scepter shall not depart from Judah, nor the lawgiver from between his feet, until Shiloh come; and unto him shall the gathering of the people be."* Jacob refers to his son Judah as a lion.

Lion is the sign for the constellation Leo. **Genesis 49** identifies Leo, the lion, and Judah with each other. Let's take a closer look at Jacob's declaration that "*the scepter shall not depart from Judah, nor a lawgiver from between his feet until Shiloh comes.*" The word for "foot" is regal. This is very significant. The star named Regulus is the brightest star in the constellation of Leo. So we have in this verse, **Genesis 49:10**, the lion of Judah, Leo, tied in with a lawgiver coming from between his feet, represented by the King Star Regulus.

To gather a clear meaning of what is being prophesied by Jacob in **Genesis 49:10**, let's take a look at **Revelation 5:5**, "*And one of the elders saith unto me, weep not: behold, the Lion of the tribe of Judah, the Root of David, hath prevailed to open the book, and to loose the seven seals thereof.*"

There it is – the conclusive link between Judah, the lion, and the Lord Jesus Christ!
The constellation Leo was the specific sign God placed in the heavens to reveal his redemptive plan – from Abraham's great-grandson, Judah, through his genealogical line to Jesus, the Christ, The Messiah. The constellation Leo is just one of many examples that demonstrate how God uses the stars as signs to reveal his divine plans to mankind.

WE HAVE SEEN HIS STAR

Matthew 2:1-2, *"Now when Jesus was born in Bethlehem of Judea in the days of Herod the King, behold, there came wise men from the east to Jerusalem, saying, where is he that is born King of the Jews? For we have seen his star in the east, and we come to worship him!"*

Matthew records in his gospel that wise men from the East traveled to Jerusalem seeking the King of the Jews, having seen his star. Isn't it interesting that no one else is on record of recognizing the celestial announcement of his birth? As far as we know, no one in all of Israel, at the time of Christ's birth, was aware of his birth through observations of the stars.

Who were these wise men, and how is it that they were able to recognize "his star"? Well, by searching what is written in the Bible and studying the astronomical evidence, we too can know and understand the truth regarding the birth of the Messiah. Let's take a quick look at who these Gentile men were, that had knowledge of God's Word, as it was revealed in the stars.

Ancient records indicate that the earliest Magi, "wise men", lived in near Eastern society, especially Persia, or in modern day Iran/Iraq. The Eastern Magi followed the teachings of Zoroaster. A close study of Zoroaster's teachings, indicate several parallels of Old Testament teachings. For example, Zoroastrians believed in one supreme God who created the heavens and the earth, and who also authored all that is good. They also believed in a spiritual adversary who authored evil. They believed in a coming redeemer, a prophet who would be sent by God to save mankind.

It has been suggested that the Magi presented their gifts to Jesus on December 25, 2 B.C. That is not correct. When the Magi arrived, Joseph and Mary were no longer in a stable with Jesus. He was not lying in a manger wrapped in swaddling clothes. According to **Matthew 2:11**, Joseph and Mary were now residing in a house. *"And when they were come into the house, they saw the young child with Mary his mother, and fell down, and worshipped him: and when they had opened their treasures, they presented unto him gifts; gold, and frankincense, and myrrh."*

Jesus had been circumcised (**Luke 2:21** *"And when eight days were accomplished for the circumcising of the child, his name was called JESUS, which was so named of the angel before he was conceived in the womb*) and dedicated at the temple some forty days after his birth. **Luke 2:22-24** *"And when the days of her purification according to the law of Moses were accomplished, they brought him to Jerusalem, to present him to the Lord; (As it written in the law of the Lord, Every male that openeth the womb shall be called holy to the Lord)."*

When the Magi arrived, Jesus was almost two years old. This is why when the Magi left, Herod had all the male children, in and around Bethlehem, who were two years of age or younger killed. **Matthew 2:16** *"Then Herod, when he saw that he was mocked of the wise men, was exceeding wroth, and sent forth, and slew all the children that were in Bethlehem, and in all the coasts thereof, from two years old and under, according to the time which he had diligently inquired of the wise men."*

EVIDENCES DATING THE BIRTH OF JESUS

The Gospel of **Luke 1:5** indicates that Herod was the king of Judaea at the time of the birth of Christ: *"there was in the days of Herod, the King of Judaea, a certain priest named Zacharias of the course of Abia, and his wife was of the daughters of Aaron, and her name was Elisabeth."*

We know Zacharias and Elisabeth were the parents of John the Baptist, the forerunner of Jesus. **Luke 1:13-17** says, *"but the angel said unto him, Fear not, Zacharias: for thy prayer is heard and thy wife Elisabeth shall bear thee a son, and thou shalt call his name John. And thou shalt have joy and gladness; and many shall rejoice at his birth. For he shall be great in the sight of the Lord, and shall drink neither wine nor strong drink; and he shall be filled with the Holy Ghost, even from his mother's womb. And many of the children of Israel shall he turn to the Lord their God. And he shall go before him in the spirit and power of Elias, to turn the hearts of the fathers to the children, and the disobedient to the wisdom of the just; to make ready a people prepared for the Lord."*

The Gospel of **Matthew 2:1** also indicates that Herod was the King of Judaea when Christ was born, *"now when Jesus was born in Bethlehem of Judea in the days of Herod the King..."* In **Luke 2:1**, we read that Caesar Augustus was the emperor of the Roman Empire, at the times of the birth of Christ... *"And it came to pass in those days, that there went out a decree from Caesar Augustus, that all the world should be taxed."*

The noted secular historian Josephus, in his highly regarded book, the *Antiquities of Jesus*, also chronicles events in Judaea at the time of the birth of Christ. Josephus mentions in his writings that an eclipse of the moon occurred shortly before Herod's death. Much scholarly debate has been centered on the time frame of Herod's death but it should be noted that all scholars concur that Herod's death occurred at some time between 7 B.C. and 1 B.C. Josephus lays out a long list of events that took place between the lunar eclipse and the observance of Passover during the year Herod died. He mentions that Herod orders the execution of two high priests during the time of a lunar eclipse.

He also points out that during this same time frame, Herod is suffering from a disease, and travels to Callirrhoe, for where he receives bath treatments, seeking relief. Herod's treatments fail, and upon his return, he gathered all the leaders of Judaea for a meeting in Jericho. When they all arrived, Herod arrested them with the intent of having them killed upon his death. During this time, he even had his own son, Antipole executed, after receiving permission from Caesar at Rome to do so. Upon his death five days later, Herod's other son, Archelaus, became King and immediately released all of the men that his father had earlier confined. Archelaus made arrangements for a huge funeral for his father. The procession was made up of Herod's soldiers and servants. Herod was buried in a fort in a mountain south of Jerusalem called the Herodian. It is reported that the funeral procession from Jericho to the Herodian took twenty-five days. Archelaus stay at Fort Herodian mourning his father for seven days and then returned to Jerusalem and made preparations to go to Rome to have Caesar officially confirm him. But a riot broke out as the Passover was beginning, so serious that Archelaus had to deploy troops to settle things down.

I believe that upon a thorough examination of the chronological events, both historically and astronomically, all of the events recorded by Josephus occurring between the lunar eclipse, and Passover, fit into a three-month time period between January and the Passover in April in the year 1 B.C.

ASTRONOMICAL EVIDENCES
DATING THE BIRTH OF JESUS

Now that we have associated with the death of King Herod that the eclipse recorded in Josephus occurred on January 9, 1 B.C., let's examine the celestial occurrences and astronomical events of that period of time. This will help us pin point the exact date and time of the actual birth of Christ.

Let us consider again **Matthew 2: 1-2** *"…behold there came wise men from the east to Jerusalem saying, where is he that is born King of the Jews? For we have seen his star in the east, and are come to worship him"*. What was it? Was it really a star? Could it have been a comet, a nova, maybe some kind of planetary conjunction, or a planet? Well, the word star as used in this passage or even in our everyday use of the word could mean any bright object in the sky. All of the research done on "his star" indicated conclusively, it was the planet Jupiter.

The planets in our solar system are referred to as wandering stars, from the Greek word *Planetes Asteres.* The object that the Magi saw was in motion. Stars on the other hand, appear to be fixed in relation to each, because they are so far out in outer space. Planets, which actually appear to us as "star type objects" move and through mathematical calculations, we can determine when planets will rise and set. Though they appear to be stars, the planets Venus, Mars, Jupiter and Saturn are visible to the naked eyes.

Little has been written regarding the significance of the planets from a Biblical perspective, but as we begin to consider planets as candidates for "his star", their spiritual significance will be realized.

Mercury, the closest planet to the sun, has long been referred to as the messenger god or one who delivers messages. The Apostle Paul, while preaching in **Acts 14:11-12**, is called Mercurius by the people of Lycaonia.

Venus, the second planet from the sun, is known for its brightness in the dawn sky. In the book of **Revelation 22:16**, Jesus is called "*the bright and morning star*".

Mars, the fourth planet from the sun, is associated with war. The Archangel Michael, the warrior, is seen protecting God's people in **Daniel 12:1** and battling the Devil in **Revelation 12:7**.

Then there's Jupiter, the largest planet in our solar system. In Hebrew, the planet Jupiter means "righteousness". Jupiter is associated with royalty. Jeremiah says in chapter twenty-three and verse five, that the Messiah who would come from David's genealogy would be the "righteous branch", and reign as King, executing righteousness. **Jeremiah 23:6** says, "*...and this is his name whereby he shall be called THE LORD OUR RIGHTEOUSNESS.*" It is clear, that the planet Jupiter has characteristics that would associate it with Jesus Christ.

Saturn, the next planet out from Jupiter, which also appears as a star like object to the naked eye, is associated with agriculture. In Judean tradition, it is identified with death, destruction, weeping and grief.

Why do I believe that Jupiter was "his star"? As the largest planet in our solar system, Jupiter was referred to by ancient astronomers as the "King Planet" – a royal planet. When we take into consideration the significant Celestine events occurring between May 27, 7 B.C., and August 27, 2 B.C., Jupiter is prominently involved.

According to astronomical records, on August 12th, in 3 B.C., at 5 A.M., Jupiter came into very close conjunction with Venus in the eastern sky. (See constellation plate - Fig. 1).

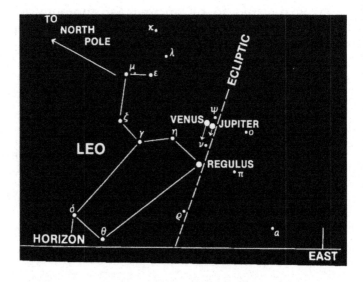

Fig. 1. Jupiter and Venus in Conjunction in Leo
5:00 A.M., August 12, 3 B.C.

This diagram shows what an observer, standing near the latitude of Palestine or Persia, would see facing east on the date August 12, 3 B.C. at 5:00 A.M. The horizontal line represents the horizon, and due east is the small vertical line marked on the horizon. Therefore, Leo at 5:00 A.M. was rising somewhat north of east. Lines connect the major stars that outline the constellation of Leo, and certain other stars are indicated for more completeness (astronomical practice marks the brighter stars in a constellation by Greek letters). The ecliptic is the path the sun moves through in its annual motion. The sun passed through Leo from July 9 until August 17 in Christ's time. Presently it moves through Leo a month later. The direction to the celestial north pole is indicated by the arrow. Arrows are drawn projecting from the planets to indicate the relative direction and speed of their motion.

This is what the Magi refer to in **Matthew 2:2**, when they said they saw it "in the rising". Let's take a close look at the spiritual significance of this. Jupiter, the planet of royalty and kingship, was in conjunction with Venus, the planet that is biblically associated with Jesus as "the bright and morning star". Astronomical records also indicate that this conjunction occurred in the constellation Leo, the sign of the lion, the constellation associated with the tribe of Judah.

As you recall from our discussion above, ASTRONOMY AND THE BIBLE, Jacob's prophecy recorded in **Genesis 49,** the Messiah was to come out of Judah as the ruler of Israel.

There we have it - on August 12, 3 B. C., the royal planet of Jupiter was in conjunction with Venus, the bright and morning star, and the constellation of Leo, representing the rulership of Judah. Now, please be mindful that the Magi did not immediately leave from Jerusalem on this appearance. There were significant conjunctions of Jupiter with other celestial bodies near the time of Christ.

On September 14, 3 B.C., Jupiter came into conjunction with the star Regulus, the brightest star of the constellation Leo. In ancient times, Regulus was known as the king star, and is identified with rulership and dominion, just like Jupiter the king planet. We think the view was similar to what was seen in August, but now Leo was high in the sky and the first stars of the constellation Virgo are beginning to rise. (see constellation plate – Fig. 2)

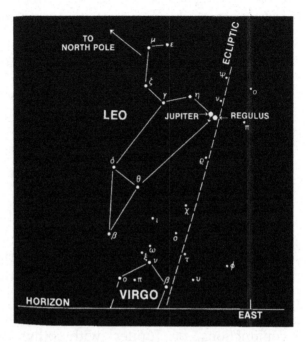

Fig. 2. Jupiter and Regulus in Conjunction in Leo
4:00 A.M., September 14, 3 B.C.

WHEN EXACTLY WAS JESUS BORN?

I am convinced that a thorough and careful examination of astronomical, historical, and biblical evidence enables us to determine precisely the date of the birth of Christ. Let us consider what is recorded by the Apostle John in **Revelation 12:1-5**, *"And there appeared a great wonder in heaven; a woman clothed with the sun, and the moon under her feet, and upon her head a crown of twelve stars: and she being with child cried, travailing in birth, and pained to be delivered. And there appeared another wonder in heaven; and behold a great red dragon, having seven heads and ten horns, and seven crowns upon his heads. And his tail drew the third part of the stars of heaven, and did cast them to the earth: and the dragon stood before the woman which was ready to be delivered, for to devour her child as soon as it was born. And she brought forth a man child, who was to rule all nations with a rod of iron: and her child was caught up unto God, and to his throne."*

Revelation 12:1 says *"there appeared a great wonder in heaven."* The word "wonder" in Greek means a sign of the Zodiac. The sign spoken of in verse one is a woman. This clearly is describing the constellation Virgo.

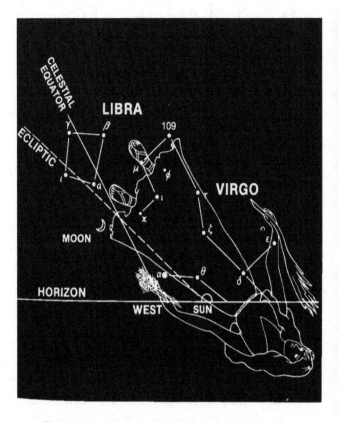

Fig. 9. The "Great Wonder" of Revelation 12:1
Sunset, 6:18 P.M., September 11, 3 B.C.

The diagram shows the sun half-way set. The sun is on the ecliptic, the dotted line, and the solid line is the celestial equator, which is directly overhead at the earth's equator. At this point, the first thin crescent of the moon appears, marking the first of the new month, Tishri.

The text goes on to say that the woman was "clothed with the sun". In the year 3 B.C., the sun was in this position from the mid-body, between the neck and the knees of the constellation Virgo, from August 27th through September 15th. Not only was the woman of **Revelation 12** "clothed with the sun", but the scripture says the moon was "under her feet". This is very significant information, because in the year 3 B.C., this occurrence with the sun and moon in Virgo take place one day only and that was September 11.

The configuration of the sun and the moon in the constellation Virgo could be seen in Palestine between sunset and moonset. On Wednesday, September 11, 3 B.C. sunset was at 6:18 PM and moonset at 7:39 PM Palestine time.

On the evening of September 11, 3 B.C., the new moon first became visible in the west shortly after sunset. The Hebrew calendar month begins on the evening that the new moon appears, so the evening of September 11th was the first day of a new month. The evening of September 11th was the first day of the seventh month of Tishri.

Jesus was born on Wednesday, September 11, 3 B.C., during the eighty-one minute span of time between 6:18 P.M. and 7:39 P.M. There is evidence that indicates Tishri was originally the first month of the Hebrew calendar. Tishri 1, Rosh Hashanah, is New Year's Day on the calendar of modern Judaism. While doing research for this booklet, I found out that, September 11th is usually the first day of the year in the Coptic and Ethiopian calendar. Interesting.........................

DECEMBER 25TH AND HIS BIRTH

How did December 25th become the most popular date in Christianity to celebrate Christ's birth? Although it has been long recognized by biblical scholars that Jesus was not born on December 25th, Christians continue to celebrate his birth on that date. December 25th is now one of the most celebrated holidays in the entire earth. Celebrating the birth of Christ on December 25th is based on tradition rather than truth. Long before the birth of Christ, many ancient cultures celebrated the birth of their sun god(s) at the time of the winter solstice in late December. The actual solstice, the tilting of the earth on its axis, occurs on December 21st. On December 25th, the sun reaches its lowest point in the southern sky, and begins to rise higher in the sky each day.

In 274 A.D., the Romans declared December 25th as the birthday of what they called the Rising Sun, or the unconquered sun - as a result of the sun beginning to noticeably show an increase in light, resulting in longer daylight hours. This festival was known as Saturnalia, or the feast of Saturn. People would decorate fir trees, the Yule log, and exchange gifts.   Festivities were characterized by wild parties, heavy drinking, even orgies usually between December 17th-24th.

In an effort to spiritualize this highly celebrated festival, the Church of Rome designated December 25th as the birth of Christ. This took place in 336 A.D. and the Church renamed the festival, "Feast of The Nativity of The Son of Righteousness". A special Mass was established for Christ and that is how we get the name Christmas – from "Christ Mass". Many of the customs of the pagans were adopted, and still observed until this day.

PROPHECIES OF THE MESSIAH FULFILLED IN JESUS CHRIST

God's promise of a Messiah, a redeemer, is the central theme of the Bible from **Genesis 3:15** to **Revelation 22:21.**

PRESENTED HERE IN THEIR ORDER OF FULFILLMENT

PROPHETIC SCRIPTURE	SUBJECT	FULFILLED
Genesis 3:15, And I will put enmity between thee and the woman, and between thy seed and her seed; it shall bruise thy head, and thou shalt bruise his heel	*seed of a woman*	*Galatians 4:4* But when the fullness of the time was come, God sent forth is Son, made of a woman, made under the law.
Genesis 12:3 And I will bless them that bless thee, and curse I'm that curseth thee: and in thee shall all families of the earth be blessed.	seed of Abraham	*Matthew 1:1* The book of the generation of Jesus Christ, the son of David, the son of Abraham.
Genesis 17:19 And God said, Sarah thy wife shall bear thee a son indeed; and thou shalt call his name Isaac: and I will establish my covenant with him for an everlasting covenant, and with his seed after him.	seed of Isaac	*Luke 3:34* Which was the son of Jacob, which was the son of Isaac, which was the son of Abraham, which was the son of Thara, which was the son of Na'-chor

Numbers 24:17 I shall see him, but not now: I shall behold him, but not nigh: there shall come a Star out of Jacob, and a Sceptre shall rise out of Israel, and shall smite the corners of Moab, and destroy all the children of Sheth.	**seed of Jacob**	**Matthew 1:2** Abraham begat Isaac; and Isaac begat Jacob; and Jacob begat Judas and his brethren;
Genesis 49:10 the sceptre shall not depart from Judah, nor a lawgiver from between his feet, until Shiloh come; and unto him shall the gathering of the people be.	**from the tribe of Judah**	**Luke 3:33** Which was the son of Aminadab, which was the son of Aram, which was the son of Esrom, which was the son of Phares, which was the son of Judah.
Isaiah 9:7 Of the increase of his government and peace there shall be no end, upon the throne of David, and upon his kingdom, to order it, and to establish it with judgment and with justice from henceforth even forever. The zeal of the Lord of hosts will perform this.	**heir to the throne of David**	**Luke 1:32, 33** He shall be great, and shall be called the Son of the Highest; and the Lord God shall give unto him the throne of his father David: And he shall reign over the house of Jacob for ever; and of his kingdom there shall be no end.

Micah 5:2 But thou, Bethlehem Ephratah, though thou be little among the thousands of Judah, yet out of thee shall he come forth unto me that is to be ruler in Israel; whose goings forth have been from of old, from everlasting.	**born in Bethlehem**	**Luke 2:4, 5, 7** And Joseph also went up from Galilee, out of the city of Nazareth, into Judaea, unto the city of David, which is called Bethlehem; (because he was of the house and lineage of David:) To be taxed with Mary his espoused wife, being great with child. And she brought forth her firstborn son, and wrapped him in swaddling clothes, and laid him in a manger; because there was no room for them in the inn.
Daniel 9:25 Know therefore and understand, that from the going forth of the commandment to restore and to build Jerusalem unto the Messiah the Prince shall be seven weeks, and threescore and two weeks the street shall be built again, and the wall, even in troublous times.	**time for His birth**	**Luke 2:1, 2** And it came to pass in those days, that there went out a decree from Caesar Augustus, that all the world should be taxed. (And this taxing was first made when Cyrenius was governor of Syria.)

		Luke 1:26, 27, 30, 31 and in the sixth month the angel Gabriel was sent from God unto a city of Galilee, named Nazareth, The a virgin espoused to a man whose name was Joseph, of the house of David; and the virgin's name was Mary. And the angel said unto her, Fear not, Mary: for thou hast found favour with God. And, behold, thou shalt conceive in thy womb, and bring forth a son, and shalt call his name JESUS.
Isaiah 7:14 therefore the Lord himself shall give you a sign; Behold, a virgin shall conceive, and bear a son, and shall call his name Immanuel.	**to be born of a virgin**	
		Matthew 2:16-18 Then Herod, when he saw that he was mocked of the wise men, was exceeding wroth, and sent forth, and slew all the children tama was there a voice heard, lamentation, and weeping and great mourning, Rachel weeping for her children, and would not be comforted because they are not.
Jeremiah 31:15 Thus saith the Lord; A voice was heard in Ramah, lamentation, and bitter weeping; Rahel weeping for her children refused to be comforted for her children, because they were not	**slaughter of the innocents**	

Hosea 11:1 When Israel was a child, then I loved him, and called my son out of Egypt.	**flight to Egypt**	*Matthew2:14* when he arose, he took the young child and his mother by night, and departed into Egypt: And was there until the death of Herod; that it might be fulfilled which was spoken of the Lord by the prophet, saying, Out of Egypt have I called my son.
Malachi 3:1 Behold, I will send my messenger, and he shall prepare the way before me: and the Lord, whom ye seek, shall suddenly come to his temple, even the messenger of the covenant, whom delight in: behold, he shall come, saith the LORD of hosts.	**preceded by a forerunner**	*Luke 7:24, 27* And when the messengers of John were departed, he began to speak unto the people concerning John, What went ye out into the wilderness for to see? This is he, of whom it is written, Behold, I send my messenger before thy face, which shall prepare they way before thee.
Psalms 2:7 I will declare the decree: the LORD hath said unto me, Thou art my son; this day have I begotten thee.	**declared the Son of God**	*Matthew 3:17* And lo a voice from heaven, saying, This is my beloved Son, in whom I am well pleased.

Isaiah 9:1 nevertheless the dimness shall not be such as was in her vexation, when at the first he lightly afflicted the land of Zebulun and the land of Naphtali, and afterward did more grievously afflict her by the way of the sea, beyond Jordan, in Galilee of the nations. The people that walked in darkness have seen a great light: they that dwell in the land of the shadow of death, upon them hath the light shined.	**Galilean ministry**	**Matthew 4:13-16**And leaving Nazareth, he came dwelt in Capernaum, which is upon the sea coast, in the borders of Zabulon and Nephthalim: That it might be fulfilled which was spoken by Esaias the prophet, saying, The land of Zabulon, and the land of Nephthalim, by the way of the sea, beyond Jordan, Galilee of the Gentiles; The people which sat in darkness saw great light; and to them which sat in the region and shadow of death light is sprung up.
Deut. 18:15 The LORD thy God will raise up unto thee a Prophet from the midst of thee, of thy brethren, like unto me; unto him ye shall hearken.	**a prophet**	**Acts 3:20**And he shall send Jesus Christ, which before was preached unto you: For Moses truly said unto the fathers, A Prophet shall the Lord your God raise up unto you of your brethren, like unto me; him shall ye hear in all things, whatsoever he shall say unto you.

Isaiah 61:1 The spirit of the Lord GOD is upon me; because the LORD hath anointed me to preach good tidings unto the meek; he hath sent me to bind up the broken-hearted, to proclaim liberty to the captives, and the opening of the prison to them that are bound; To proclaim the acceptable year of the LORD, and the day of vengeance of our God; to comfort all that mourn;	**to heal the broken-hearted**	*Luke 4:18* The Spirit of the Lord is upon me, because he hat anointed me to preach the gospel to the poor; he hath sent me to heal the brokenhearted, to preach deliverance to the captives, and recovering of sight to the blind, to set at liberty them that are bruised, To preach the acceptable year of the Lord.
Isaiah 53:3 He is despised and rejected of men; a man of sorrows, and acquainted with grief: and we hid as it were our faces from him; he was despised, and we esteemed him not.	**rejected by his own people, the Jews**	*John 1:11* He came unto his own, and his own received him not. *Luke 23:18* And they cried out all at once, saying, Away with this man, and release unto us Barabbas;

Psalms 110:4 the LORD hath sworn, and will not repent, Thou art a priest forever after the order of Melchizedek.	**priest after order of Melchizedek**	**Hebrew 5:5** So also Christ glorified not himself to be made an high priest; but he that said unto him, Thou art my Son, today have I begotten thee. As he saith also in another place, thou art a priest for ever after the order of Melchisedec.
Zech. 9:9 greatly, O daughter of Zion; shout, O daughter of Jerusalem: behold, thy King cometh unto thee: he is just, and having salvation; lowly, and riding upon an ass, and upon a colt the foal of an ass.	**triumphal entry**	**Mark 11:7, 9, 11** And they brought the colt to Jesus, and cast their garments on him; and he sat upon him. And they that went before, and they that followed, cried, saying, Hosanna; Blessed is he that cometh in the name of the Lord: And Jesus entered into Jerusalem, and into the temple: and when he had looked round about upon all things, and now the eventide was come, he went out unto Bethany with the twelve.

Psalms 41:9 Yea, mine own familiar friend, in whom I trusted, which did eat of my bread, hath lifted up his heel against me.	**betrayed by a friend**	*Luke 22:47, 48* And while he yet spake, behold a multitude, and he that was called Judas, one of the twelve, went before them, and drew near unto Jesus to kiss him. But Jesus said unto him, Judas, betrayest thou the Son of man with a kiss?
Zech. 11:12 And I said unto them, if ye think good, give me my price; and if not, forbear. So they weighed for my price thirty pieces of silver.	**sold for thirty pieces of silver**	*Matt 26:15* And said unto them, What will ye give me, and I will deliver him unto you? And they covenanted with him for thirty pieces of silver.
Psalms 35:11 False witnesses did rise up; they laid to my charge things that I knew not.	**accused by false witnesses**	Mark 14:57, 58 And there arose certain, and bare false witness against him, saying, We heard him say, I will destroy this temple that is made with hands, and within three days I will build another made without hands.

Isaiah 53:7 He was oppressed, and he was afflicted, yet he opened not his mouth: he is brought as a lamb to the slaughter, and as a sheep before her shearers is dumb, so he openeth not his mouth.	**silent to accusations**	*Mark 15:4, 5*And Pilate asked him again, saying, Answerest thou nothing? Behold how many things they witness against thee. But Jesus yet answered nothing; so that Pilate marveled.
Isaiah 50:6 I gave my back to the smiters, and my cheeks to them that plucked off the hair: I hid not my face from shame and spitting.	**spat upon and smitten**	*John 1:11* He came unto his own, and his own received him not. Luke 23:18 And they cried out all at once, saying, Away with this man, and release unto us Barabbas;
*Psalms 35:19*Let not them that are mine enemies wrongfully rejoice over me: neither let them wink with the eye that hates me without a cause.	**hated without reason**	*John 15:24, 25* If I had not done among them the works which none other man did, they had not had sin: but now have they both seen and hated both me and my Father. But this cometh to pass, that the word might be fulfilled that is written in their law, They hated me without a cause.

Isaiah 53:5 But he was wounded for our transgressions, he was bruised for our iniquities: the chastisement of our peace was upon him; and with his stripes we are healed.	**vicarious sacrifice**	*Romans 5:6, 8* for when we were yet without strength, in due time Christ died for the ungodly. But God commendeth his love toward us, in that, while we were yet sinners, Christ died for us.
Isaiah 53:12 Therefore will I divide him a portion with the great, and he shall divide the spoil with the strong; because he hath poured out his soul unto death: and he was numbered with the transgressors; and he bare the sin of many, and made intercession for the transgressors.	**crucified with malefactors**	*Mark 15:27, 28* And with him they crucify two thieves; the one on his right hand, and the other on his left. And the scripture was fulfilled, which saith, and he was numbered with the transgressors.

Zech.12:10 And I will pour upon the house of David, and upon the inhabitants of Jerusalem, the spirit of grace and of supplications: and they shall look upon me whom they have pierced, and they shall mourn for him, as one mourneth for his only son, and shall be in bitterness for him, as one that is in bitterness for his firstborn.	**pierced through hands and feet**	*John 20:27* Then saith he to Thomas, Reach hither thy finger, and behold my hands; and reach hither thy hand, and thrust it into my side: and be not faithless, but believing.
Psalms 22:7 All they that see me laugh me to scorn: they shoot out the lip, they shake the head, saying, He trusted upon the LORD that he would deliver him: let him deliver him, seeing he delighted in him.	**scorned and mocked**	*Luke 23:35* And the people stood beholding. And the rulers also with them derided him, saying, He saved others; let him save himself, if he be Christ, the chosen of God.
Psalms 69:12 They gave me also gall for my meat; and in my thirst they gave me vinegar to drink.	**given vinegar and gall**	*Matthew 27:34* They gave vinegar to drink mingled with gall; and when he had tasted thereof, he would not drink.

Psalms 109:4 For my love they are my adversaries; but I give myself unto prayer.	**prayer for his enemies**	*Luke 23:34* Then said Jesus, Father, forgive them; for they know not what they do. And they parted his raiment, and cast lots.
Psalms 22:17, 18 I may tell all my bones; they look and stare upon me. They part my garments among them, and cast lots upon vesture.	**soldiers gambled for his coat**	*Matthew 27:35* And they crucified him, and parted his garments, casting lots: that it might be fulfilled which was spoken by the prophet, They parted my garments among them, and upon my vesture did they cast lots. And sitting down they watched him there;
Psalms 34:20 He keepeth all his bones; not one of them is broken.	**no bone broken**	*John 19:32, 33, 36* Then came the soldiers, and brake the legs of the first, and of the other which was crucified with him. But when they came to Jesus, and saw that he was dead already, they break not his legs: For these things were done that the scripture should be fulfilled, A bone of him shall not be broken.

Zech 12:10 And I will pour upon the house of David, and upon the inhabitants of Jerusalem, they spirit of grace and of supplications: and they shall look upon me whom they have pierced, and they shall mourn for him, as one mourneth for his only son, and shall be in bitterness for him, as one that is in bitterness for his firstborn.	**his side pierced**	**John 19:34** But one of the soldiers with a spear pierced his side, and forth with came there out blood and water.

		Matthew 27:57-60 when the even was come, there came a rich man of Arimathaea, named Joseph, who also himself was Jesus' disciple: He went to Pilate, and begged the body of Jesus. Then Pilate commanded the body to be delivered. And when Joseph had taken the body, he wrapped it in a clean linen cloth, And it laid it in his own new tomb, which he had hewn out in the rock: and he rolled a great stone to the door of the sepulcher, and departed.
Isaiah 53:9 And he made his grave with the wicked, and with the rich in his death; because he had done no violence, neither was any deceit in his mouth.	**buried with the rich**	

Psalms 16:10 For thou wilt not leave my soul in hell; neither wilt thou suffer thine Holy One to see corruption. *Psalms 49:15* But God will redeem my soul from the power of the grave: for he shall receive me. Selah.	**to be resurrected**	*Mark 16:6, 7* ...and he saith unto them, Be not affrighted: ye seek Jesus of Nazareth, which was crucified: he is risen; he is not here: behold the place where they laid him. But go your way, tell his disciples and Peter that he goeth before you into Galilee: there shall ye see him, as he said unto you.
Psalms 68:18 Thou hast ascended on high, thou hast led captivity captive: thou hast received gifts for men; yea, for the rebellious also, that the LORD God might dwell among them.	**His ascension to God's right hand**	*Mark 16:19* So then after the Lord had spoken unto them, he was received up into heaven, and sat on the right hand of God. *1 Cor. 15:4* And that he was buried, and that he rose again the third day according to the scriptures: *Ephesians 4:8* Wherefore he saith, When he ascended up on high, he led captivity captive, and gave gifts unto men.

CALENDAR OF MAJOR EVENTS FROM
4 B.C. TO 1 B.C

Hebrew Month		Roman Month	
TEBETH	30	JANUARY	31
SHEBAT	30	FEBRUARY	28
ADAR	29	MARCH	31
NISAN	30	APRIL	30
IYYAR	29	MAY	31
SIVAN	30	JUNE	30
TAMMUZ	29	JULY	31
AB	30	AUGUST	31
ELUL	29	SEPTEMBER	30
TISHRI	30	OCTOBER	1
MARCHESHVAN	29	NOVEMBER	30
KISLEV	30	DECEMBER	31
TEBETH	29		

Passover

April 12-19

Course of Abia

May 26—June 2

Elisabeth Conceives

Elisabeth's 6th Month of Pregnancy

Gabriel Appears to Mary

4 B.C.

CALENDAR OF MAJOR EVENTS
4 B.C. TO 1 B.C

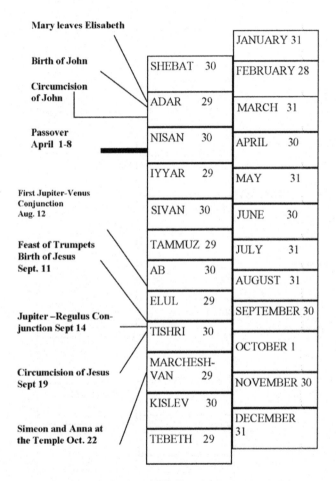

Mary leaves Elisabeth

Birth of John

Circumcision
of John

Passover
April 1-8

First Jupiter-Venus
Conjunction
Aug. 12

Feast of Trumpets
Birth of Jesus
Sept. 11

Jupiter –Regulus Con-
junction Sept 14

Circumcision of Jesus
Sept 19

Simeon and Anna at
the Temple Oct. 22

		JANUARY 31
SHEBAT	30	FEBRUARY 28
ADAR	29	MARCH 31
NISAN	30	APRIL 30
IYYAR	29	MAY 31
SIVAN	30	JUNE 30
TAMMUZ	29	JULY 31
AB	30	AUGUST 31
ELUL	29	SEPTEMBER 30
TISHRI	30	OCTOBER 1
MARCHESH-VAN	29	NOVEMBER 30
KISLEV	30	DECEMBER 31
TEBETH	29	

3 B.C.

CALENDAR OF MAJOR EVENTS FROM 4 B.C. TO 1 B.C

Hebrew Month	Roman Month
SHEBAT 30	JANUARY 31
ADAR 29	FEBRUARY 28
ADAR II 30	MARCH 31
NISAN 29	APRIL 30
IYYAR 30	MAY 31
SIVAN 29	JUNE 30
TAMMUZ 30	JULY 31
AB 29	AUGUST 31
ELUL 30	SEPTEMBER 30
TISHRI 30	OCTOBER 1
MARCHESH-VAN 30	NOVEMBER 30
KISLEV 29	DECEMBER 31

Jupiter—Regulus Conjunction Feb 17

Passover April 20-17

Jupiter—Regulus Conjunction May 8

Last Jupiter – Regulus Conjunction June 17

Massing of Planets in Leo Aug 27

Jupiter on Meridian Dec 4

**Hanukkah Dec. 24-31
Arrival of Magi in Bethlehem
Joseph, Mary, Jesus flee to Egypt**

2 B.C.

CALENDAR OF MAJOR EVENTS FROM
4 B.C. TO 1 B.C

Lunar Eclipse *(→)*	TEBETH 30	JANUARY 31

**Lunar Eclipse
before Herod's
Death
January 9**

**Archelaus Disrupts
Passover April 8
Joseph, Mary, Jesus
return to Nazareth**

Hebrew Month	Gregorian Month
TEBETH 30	JANUARY 31
SHEBAT 29	FEBRUARY 28
ADAR 29	MARCH 31
NISAN 30	APRIL 30
IYYAR 29	MAY 31
SIVAN 30	JUNE 30
TAMMUZ 29	JULY 31
AB 30	AUGUST 31
ELUL 29	SEPTEMBER 30
TISHRI 30	OCTOBER 1
MARCHESH-VAN 30	NOVEMBER 30
KISLEV 30	DECEMBER 31

1 B.C.

Events surrounding the birth of Christ can be historically and/or astronomically pinpointed.

May, 4 B.C.	During the course of Abia, the angel Gabriel appears to Zacharias serving in the Temple
June, 4 B.C.	Conception of John the Baptist
Dec. 4 B.C.	Gabriel appears to Mary in Nazareth; conception of Jesus Christ; Mary travels to Judea to see her cousin Elisabeth
March 3 B.C.	Mary returns to Nazareth; John the Baptist is born to Zacharias and Elisabeth
Aug. 12, 3B.C.	Jupiter and Venus in conjunction in Leo; Magi begin noting their observations of the activity of Jupiter, the king planet
Sept. 11, 3 B.C.	Birth of Jesus Christ; first day of Tishri; sun in Virgo with the "moon under her feet"

Sept. 14, 3 B.C.	Jupiter and Regulus in conjunction in Leo
Feb. 17, 2 B.C.	Jupiter and Regulus in conjunction in Leo
May 8, 2 B.C.	Jupiter and Regulus in conjunction in Leo
June 17, 2 B.C.	Jupiter and Regulus in conjunction in Leo
Aug. 27, 2 B.C.	massing of planets Jupiter, Mars, mercury, and Venus in Leo; Jupiter and Mars in conjunction; Magi leave for Jerusalem after this celestial event
Dec. 2 B.C.	Magi arrive in Jerusalem; Jupiter visible over Bethlehem before dawn as the Magi travel there to worship the Christ who is more than one year and three months old; Magi depart from Persia; Joseph, Mary, and Jesus flee to Egypt
Jan. 9, 1 B.C.	Archelaus, the new king of Judea, disrupts Passover; Joseph, Mary, and Jesus returning to Judea from Egypt "turn aside" into Galilee and settle in Nazareth

Biblical Passages

Listed below are the Bible verses surrounding the birth of Christ in the order in which they occurred.

Luke 1:5-25	Angel's announcement to Zacharias in the Temple of the birth of John the Baptist
Luke 1:26-38	Angel's announcement of the birth of Jesus to Mary in Nazareth
Luke 1:39-56	Mary visits her cousin Elisabeth, mother of John the Baptist, for three months
Luke 1:57-80	Birth of John the Baptist to Zacharias and Elisabeth
Matt. 1:18-24	Joseph is encouraged by an angel of the Lord "to take unto thee Mary thy wife"
Matt. 1:25a;	Jesus Christ is born in Bethlehem
Luke 2:1-20	
Matt. 1:25b;	Jesus' circumcision and naming
Luke 2:21	
Luke 2:22-24	Mary's purification and Jesus' presentation to the Lord

Eternity with God

This book has tried to show you beyond all doubt not only the exact date that Jesus was born, but also that He is the Son of God, the Promised Messiah. Jesus taught us much about the afterlife. As the only person to ever leave eternity to come to earth, to go back to eternity, Jesus knows the whole truth.   He wants us to have understanding, so that we know how to prepare. In all of His teachings, Jesus identified only two possible locations in the afterlife, heaven or hell. Both last forever. Think about it, most of our life – happens after physical death.

I want to show you a picture that will help you put eternity into perspective. See the dot and the line below?

•
_____

The dot is small and exists in one little place. The line begins in one place then takes off across the page. Imagine that the line extends off the page, and goes on, and on, and on without end. The dot stands for your whole life here on earth. The line represents your life after death in eternity- that's forever, and ever. Jesus taught us that what happens inside the dot determines everything that happens on the line. One small choice on the dot can make a big difference on the line. Would you say that you have been living for the line or for the dot? Jesus came to show you how you can change your future beginning with one small choice.

If you have been reading this book, and you are not sure where you will spend eternity, please allow me to ask you a question. Do you have a personal relationship with Jesus Christ? Have you ever confessed faith in Him as your personal Lord and Savior?

This is a prayer that God always answers, and is delighted to hear.

"Heavenly Father, have mercy on me, I am a sinner. I believe in you and that your word is true. I believe that Jesus Christ is the Son of the living God and that he died on the cross so that I may now have forgiveness for my sins and eternal life. I know that without you in my heart my life is meaningless.

I believe in my heart that you, Lord God, raised Him from the dead. Please Lord Jesus forgive me, and come into my heart as my personal Lord and Savior today.

Amen.

APPENDIX 1 - Scriptures that show Jesus Christ as our Sin Bearer

Isaiah 53 v 6: *We all, like sheep, have gone astray, each of us has turned to his own way; and the Lord has laid on him the iniquity of us all.*

1 Peter 2 v 24: *He himself bore our sins in his body on the tree, so that we might die to sins and live for righteousness; by his wounds you have been healed.*

Isaiah 53 v 12: *Therefore I will give him a portion among the great, and he will divide the spoils with the strong, because he poured out his life unto death, and was numbered with the transgressors. For he bore the sin of many and made intercession for the transgressors.*

Hebrews 9 v 28: *So Christ was sacrificed once to take away the sins of many people; and he will appear a second time, not to bear sin, but to bring salvation to those who are waiting for him.*

1 John 2 v 2: *He is the atoning sacrifice for our sins, and not only for ours but also for the sins of the whole world.*

1 John 3 v 5: *But you know that he appeared so that he might take away our sins. And in him is no sin.*

Galatians 3 v 13: *Christ redeemed us from the curse of the law by becoming a curse for us, for it is written: "Cursed is everyone who is hung on a tree."*

1 John 4 v 10: *This is love: not that we loved God, but that he loved us and sent his son as an atoning sacrifice for our sins.*

Isaiah 53 v 5: *But he was pierced for our transgressions, he was crushed for our iniquities; the punishment that brought us peace was upon him, and by his wounds we are healed.*

Hebrews 2 v 9: *But we see Jesus, who was made a little lower than the angels, now crowned with glory and honor because he suffered death, so that by the grace of God he might taste death for everyone.*

1 Peter 3 v 18: *For Christ died for sins once for all, the righteous for the unrighteous, to bring you to God. He was put to death in the body but made alive by the spirit.*

Ephesians 1 v 7: *In Him we have redemption through his blood, the forgiveness of sins, in accordance with the riches of God's grace.*

Romans 5 v 6- 11: *(6) You see, at just the right time, when we were still powerless, Christ died for the ungodly. (7) Very rarely will anyone die for a righteous man, though for a good man someone might possibly dare to die. (8) But God demonstrates his own love for us in this: While we were still sinners, Christ* died for us. *(9) Since we have been justified by his blood, how much more shall we be saved from God's wrath through him! (10) For if, when we were God's enemies, we were reconciled to him through the death of his Son, how much more, having been reconciled, shall we be saved through his life! (11) Not only is this so, but we also rejoice in God through our Lord Jesus Christ, through whom we have now received reconciliation.*

Galatians 1 v 4: *Who gave himself for our sins to rescue us from the present evil age, according to the will of our God and Father.*

Ephesians 5 v 2: *And live a life of love, just as Christ loved us and gave himself up for us and gave himself for us as a fragrant offering and sacrifice to God.*

Titus 2 v 14: *(v13) Jesus Christ, (14) who gave himself for us to redeem us from all wickedness and to purify for himself a people that are his very own, eager to do what is good.*

1 John 3 v 16: *This is how we know what love is: Jesus Christ laid down his life for us. And we ought to lay down our lives for our brothers.*

Revelation 1 v 5: *And from Jesus Christ, who is the faithful witness, the firstborn from the dead, and the ruler of kings of the earth. To him who loves us and has freed us from our sins by his blood.*

Matthew 1 v 21: *She will give birth to a son, and you are to give him the name Jesus, because he will save his people from their sins.*

2 Corinthians 5 v 21: *God made him who had no sin to be sin for us, so that in him we might become the righteousness of God.*

Ephesians 2 v 1- 9: *(1) As for you, you were dead in your transgressions and sins, (2) in which you used to live when you followed the ways of the world and of the ruler of the kingdom of the air, the spirit who is now at work in those who are disobedient. (3) All of us also lived among them at one time, gratifying the cravings of our sinful nature and following it's desires and thoughts. Like the rest, we were by nature objects of wrath. (4) But because of his great love for us, God, who is rich in mercy, (5) made us alive with Christ even when we were dead in transgressions –it is by grace you have been saved. (6) And God raised us up with Christ and seated us with him in the heavenly realms in Christ Jesus, (7) in order that in the coming ages he might show the incomparable riches of his grace, expressed in his kindness to us in Christ Jesus. (8) For it is by grace you have been saved, through faith –and this not from yourselves, it is the gift of God- (9) not by works, so that no one can boast.*

Hebrews 2 v 14- 17: *(14) Since children have flesh and blood, he too shared in their humanity so that by his death he might destroy him who holds the power* *of death –that is, the devil –(15) and free those who all their lives were held in slavery by their fear of death. (16) For surely it is not angels he helps, but Abraham's descendants. (17) For this reason he had to be made like his brothers in every way, in order that he might become a merciful and faithful high priest in service to God, and that he might make atonement for the sins of the people.*

APPENDIX 2 (Constellation Plates)

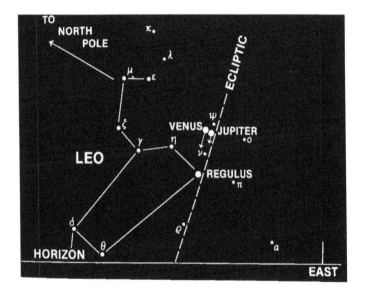

Fig. 1. Jupiter and Venus in Conjunction in Leo
5:00 A.M., August 12, 3 B.C.

This diagram shows what an observer, standing near the latitude of Palestine or Persia, would see facing east on the date August 12, 3 B.C. at 5:00 A.M. The horizontal line represents the horizon, and due east is the small vertical line marked on the horizon. Therefore, Leo at 5:00 A.M. was rising somewhat north of east. Lines connect the major stars that outline the constellation of Leo, and certain other stars are indicated for more completeness (astronomical practice marks the brighter stars in a constellation by Greek letters). The ecliptic is the path the sun moves through in its annual motion. The sun passed through Leo from July 9 until August 17 in Christ's time. Presently it moves through Leo a month later. The direction to the celestial north pole is indicated by the arrow. Arrows are drawn projecting from the planets to indicate the relative direction and speed of their motion.

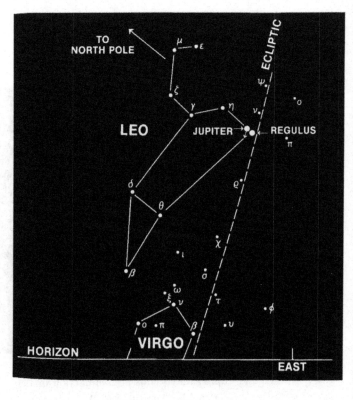

Fig. 2. Jupiter and Regulus in Conjunction in Leo
4:00 A.M., September 14, 3 B.C.

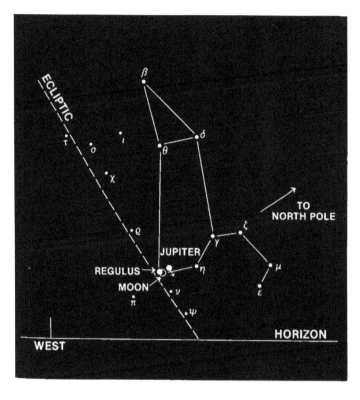

Fig. 3. Jupiter and Regulus in Conjunction in Leo
4:30 A.M., February 17, 2 B.C.

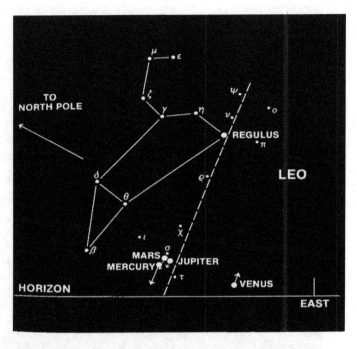

Fig. 6. Massing of Planets Jupiter, Mars, Mercury, and
Venus in Leo (Jupiter and Mars in Conjunction)
5:00 A.M., August 27, 2 B.C.

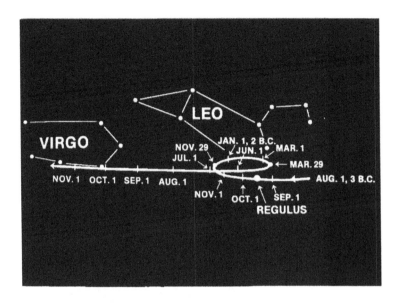

Fig. 7. Path of Jupiter
August, 3 B.C.—November, 2 B.C.

Expanded vertical scale to indicate retrograde motion.

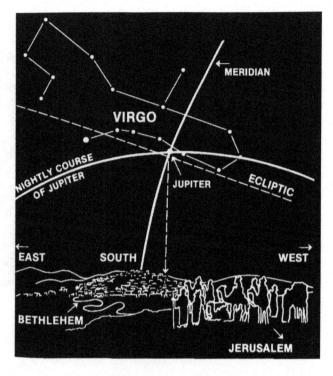

Fig. 8. Magi Approach Bethlehem
6:30 A.M., December, 2 B.C.

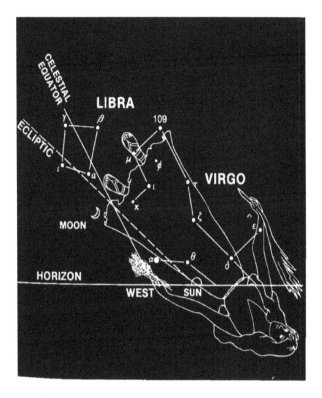

Fig. 9. The "Great Wonder" of Revelation 12:1
Sunset, 6:18 P.M., September 11, 3 B.C.

The diagram shows the sun half-way set. The sun is on the ecliptic, the dotted line, and the solid line is the celestial equator, which is directly overhead at the earth's equator. At this point, the first thin crescent of the moon appears, marking the first of the new month, Tishri.

Notes

1. Akaria, A. A. *Calendar for 6000 years: Comparative Calendar of All Chronological Tables from the Creation Until the End of the Sixth Millennium.* Jerusalem: Mossad Harav Kook, 1075.

2. Allen, Richard Hinckley. *Star names: Their Lore and Meaning.* 1899. New ed. New York: Dover Publications 1963.

3. Barnes, T. D. "The Date of Herod's Death." *Journal of Theological Studies* 19(1968): 204-209.

4. Bruce, F. F. "Review of the Birth of Christ Recalculate!" *The Evangelical Quarterly 12* (1980): 64.

5. Carter, G. W. *Zoroastrianism and Judaism.* New York: AMS Press, 1970.

6. Ciotti, Joseph. "The Magi's Star: Misconceptions and New Suggestions." *Griffith Observer,* December 1978, pp. 2-14.

7. Dobin, Joel C. *To Rule Both Day and Night: Astrology in the Bible, Midrash, and Talmud.* New York: Inner Traditions International, 1977.

8. Ferguson, Clyde L. *The Stars and the Bible.* Hicksville, N. Y.: Exposition Press, 1978.

9. Goldstine, Herman H. "New and Full Moons One Thousand and One B. C. to A. D. Sixteen Fifty One." *American Philosophical Society: Memoirs* 94 (1973).

10. Hodson, F. R., ed. *The Place of Astronomy in the Ancient World.* Organized by D. G. Kendall, S. Piggott, D. G. King-Hele, and I. E. S. Edwards. London: Oxford University Press, 1974.

11. Hughes, D. W. "The Star of Bethlehem". *Nature,* December 1976, pp. 513-517.

12. Kastner, Sidney O. "Calculations of the Twilight Visibility Function of the Near-Sun Objects." *The Journal of the Royal Astronomical Society of Canada* 70 (1976): 153-168.

13. Kudlek, Manfred, and Mickler, Erich H. *Solar and Lunar Eclipses of the Ancient East from 3000 B. C. to 0 with Maps.* Neukirchener Verlag des Erziehungsvereins Neukirchen-Vluyn: Verlag Butzon & Bercker Kevelaer, 1971.

14. Lundmark, K. "The Messianic Ideas and Their Astronomical Background." *Actes du vii congres international d'histoire des sciences, Jerusalem* 4 (1953): 436-439.

15. ____. "Suspected new Stars Recorded in Old Chronicles and Among Recent Meridian Observations." *Publications of the Astronomical Society of the Pacific* 33 (October 1931): 225-238.

16. Marshall, Roy K. *The Star of Bethlehem.* Chapel Hill, N. C.: Morehead Planetarium, 1949.

17. ____. "Star of Bethlehem?" *Sky and Telescope,* December 1943, p. 15.

18. Martin, Ernest L. (*Additional) Supplement to the Book Birth of Christ Recalculated.* 2d ed. Pasadena: Foundation for Biblical Research, 1980.

19. ____. *The Birth of Christ Recalculated.* 2d ed. Pasadena: Foundation for Biblical Research, 1980.

20. ____. "The Birth of Christ Recalculated! – Revised" *The Foundation Commentator,* June 1980, pp. 7-12.

21. ____. "The Celestial Pageantry Dating Christ's Birth." *Christianity Today,* 3 December 1976, pp. 16-18.

22. Mosley, John, and Martin, Ernest L. "The Star of Bethlehem Reconsidered: An Historical Approach." *Planetarium*, Summer 1980, pp. 6-9.

23. Norton, Arthur P. *Norton's Star Atlas and Reference Handbook.* 16th ed. Revised and edited. Cambridge, Mass.: Sky Publishing Co., 1973.

24. Nweeya, Samuel K. *Persia: The Land of the Magi.* 5th ed. Rev. Philadelphia: John C. Winston, 1913.

25. Pritchard, Charles. "On the Conjunctions of the Planets Jupiter and Saturn in the Years B. C. 66, and A. D. 54." *Royal Astronomical Society: Memoirs* 25 (1857): 119-123.

26. Rand, Howard B. *The Stars Declare God's Handiwork.* Merrimac, Mass.: Destiny, 1944.

27. Rodman, Robert. "A Linguistic note on the Christmas Star." *Griffith Observer,* December 1976, pp. 8-9.

28. Rosenberg, Roy A. "The 'Star of the Messiah' Reconsidered." *Biblica 53* (1972): 105-109.

29. Schurer, Emil. *The History of the Jewish People in the Age of Jesus Christ.* 2 vols. Revised and edited by Geza Vermes, Fergus Millar, and Matthew Black. Edinburgh: T. & T. Clark, 1973-1979.

30. Seiss, Joseph A. *The Gospel in the Stars.* 1882, Illus. ed. Grand Rapids: Kregel, 1972.

31. Silver, A. H. *A History of Messianic speculation in Israel.* Boston: Beacon Press, 1927.

32. Sinnott, Roger W. "Thoughts on the star of Bethlehem." *Sky and Telescope,* December 1968, pp. 384-386.

33. Stahlman, William D., and Gingerich, Owen. *Solar and Planetary Longitudes for Years -2500 to +2000 by 10-Day Intervals.* Madison: University of Wisconsin Press, 1963.

34. Thorley, John. ["Review of *The Birth of Christ Recalculated!"]. Joint Association of Classical Teachers: Bulletin,* November 1979.

35. Tuckerman, Bryant. *Planetary, Lunar, and Solar Positions: 601 B. C. to A. D. 1969 at Five-Day and Ten-Day Intervals.* 2 vols. Philadelphia: American Philosophical Society, 1962.

36. Van Goudoever, J. *Biblical Calendars.* Leiden: E. J. Brill, 1959.

37. Wenning, Carl J. "The Star of Bethlehem Reconsidered: A Theological Approach." *Planetarium,* Summer 1980, p. 2.

38. Whiston, William, trans. *Josephus: Complete Works.* Reprint. Grand Rapids: Kregel, 1960.

39. Wierwill, Victor Paul. *Jesus Christ, Our Promised Seed.* American Christian Press, 1982.

40. Williams, J. *Observations of Comets from B. C. 611 to A. D. 1640.* London: Strangeways and Walden, 1871.

Made in the USA
Las Vegas, NV
05 November 2022

58785291R00046